ANTHEMS IN THE GLORIOUS DAWN

Kalu Onwuka

𝕲𝕻

Granada Publishers

Los Angeles, California

Anthems in the Glorious Dawn

Copyright © 2013 by Kalu Onwuka

This title is published in Los Angeles, California by Granada Publishers using the Granada Publishing imprint. Granada Publishers is wholly owned by Granada Publishing Company, Los Angeles, California.

Granada Publishing titles may be purchased in bulk for educational, business, fundraising or sales promotional use. For more information please e-mail **sales@granadapublishing.com**

Library of Congress Cataloging-in-Publication Data

Anthems in the Glorious Dawn / Kalu Onwuka

LCCN-2013919827

ISBN: 978-0-9900203-0-1

ISBN: 0-9900203-0-4

Printed in the United States

Dedication

⚜

I will like to dedicate this book to my late parents (Onwuka and Mabel) who taught me that there is contentment in the little with God as well as to all the saintly souls who labor in relative obscurity in their 'little' lots on earth to share God's truth, light and love. You may seem little in the eyes of the world but rejoice in that the heavenly Father who is ever faithful has promised to exalt all such as you in due time.

Acknowledgments

I will first like to acknowledge Christ Jesus as the Lord of my life. He is my muse and I write because his Spirit enables me to. I will also like to acknowledge everyone who contributed to this endeavor either directly or indirectly especially my wife Nena, children Mabel, Margaret, Chioma, Charles and Christopher. Remember that life is a great teacher and blesses those who heed her lessons well. May you always be guided in love to rally to the cause of goodness, mercy and justice.

CONTENTS

CONTENTS

CONTENTS

❧

CONTENTS

CONTENTS

CONTENTS

OTHER BOOKS BY KALU ONWUKA INCLUDE-

꧁꧂

(Poetry)

In Enchantment of Eternity

Capsules of Divine Splendor

Tones of the Stellar

(Books for Spirit, Mind and Body)

Nuggets of Resurrection

Pulses of the Divine Heart

Etching for the Faithful Heart

No Hurry to Horeb

(Quotations and Insights)

Inspiration Fountain

All titles are available as paperbacks or e-books and may be purchased through many retail outlets/distribution channels. All titles may also be purchased through Granada Publishers at **granadapublishing.com.** In addition, excerpts of the author's works can be read through his website at **kaluonwuka.com.**

FOREWORD

This book titled *Anthems in the Glorious Dawn* is a compilation of original poems and songs that frame the author's spiritual as well as worldly experiences. It is really a book of testimony that speaks about places that must be left behind in order for man to find the better in his future.

There are ninety-three original poems in this volume that are wide ranging and tell compelling stories. There is an underlying stream that runs through the verses and pools them together in a way that makes for ease of reading. The poetic stream courses through such refreshing pools as excellence that is found in freedom, strong faith that exalts in life, whispers of love to soothe the heart, beauty of wisdom as a well-fitting attire and reconfiguration of spirit needed to treasure the precious in life.

Each pool of verses follows a particular vein that offers a unique perspective while encouraging readers of all faith to seek out the truth therein and reconnect with the divine. The book makes for an interesting reading that the perceptive person will find to be enriching and spiritually uplifting. It is a gem for all who love poetry and the ever-lasting beauty of simple words fitly spoken.

Kalu Onwuka

Ode to the Divine

You have brought me into marvelous light

The darkness and shadows have receded

You have given me a sunny snapshot of life

What I have long desired and yet will have

Yes, all that ail me are now fleeing

You have led me to the stream of living water

Where my parched soul will be refreshed

As I kneel down to drink with humble thanks

Pure water that flows from the divine throne

Yes, all that ail me are now fleeing

I have tarried with hope on the strait path

Seemingly alone but kept along through faith

You have led me to the Parkway of mercy

To cherish and amaze at what grace can avail

Yes, all that ailed me have now fled!

End

Gardeners of Eden

Due changes and transformation

As the faithful rally to the cause

With much of humanity still left

To be rescued before time's end

Little love for the way of light

Excessive lust for the world's way

Alive in body but dead in spirit

Strangers all who know not Creator

The vanguard of hope on earth

With hearts set on the noble task

Thru all seasons and in all hours

Labor to sow the seeds of change

Gardeners of Eden (Cont'd)

By collective impetus through grace

In good wishes and ardent prayers

The saintly are ordained in full light

To be catalysts to change humanity

They are the gardeners of new Eden

Who prune life's weeds with prayers

The cares and worries of the world

Such that choke all the earthly souls

They speak with the needed urgency

In little tweets and in real time

Do keep love's divine appointment

Eden's gardeners plead with all men

End

~ 4 ~

Hope's Sojourners

The sons of light take certain paths

With purposed steps guided by love

In a purer and greater illumination

As they complete the earthly route

With power to pray for forgiveness

And healing for benefit of mankind

Much good comes about wherever

Hope's sojourners find due welcome

Vessels to offer prayers from below

And receive blessings from above

Must keep their hearts' doors open

In compassion for the needs of men

❦

Afflictions and pain visit sometimes

As they share in the burden of others

And appropriate God's divine power

To do the marvelous in men's lives

Father always searches their hearts

In answer to petitions and requests

All in kindness through Providence

To afford the needed in timely order

Hearts set on the pure and lovely

Vessels meet for the works of glory

Things worthy of that good report

In such are Hope's sojourners found

End

Highway of the Free

The vessels of mercy forgive all
Harbor no resentments for men
Including the good and the bad
Make no distinction 'tween them

The channel of mercy is forever
A freeway for the lovely in life
Where goodness and mercy flow
With nothing to choke their path

Tis highway of the free in spirit
For only noble souls to traverse
Riders in high and exalted places
Who have overcome the world

They let go of emotional malware

That drags the spirit into a stall

So they can soar like eagle spirits

Above where there's no stagnation

The stalled spirit is unable to ride

On the high but the lowly places

Lost his esteemed place of honor

A chance to walk among the 'gods'

Man's past is laden with mistakes

That weigh down his spirit in dust

The imperfect past is left behind

To attain the future full of promise

✦

The man that seeks for life's better

Must bid goodbye to the dark past

Say farewell to the night of the old

So as to awake in dawn of the new

He must forgive and bless in love

With no judgments and vengeance

So heaven's window can open wide

For fortune's face to smile on him

End

Gift of Mercy

The path of mercy is golden
Higher than man's earthly ways
It is the highway of the noble
Given to walk in heavenly steps

Mercy is given freely and fully
To the faithful who wait in hope
A divine gift that gently alights
Comes with no strings attached

Mercy is the place of last resort
For beyond is nothing but despair
No place in mercy for superiority
But ample room for importunity

Mercy is the difference between

Rebirth and the eclipse of hope

It is the lifeline for the drowning

The flicker of light in a dark sea

The power of mercy always lead

Wicked men to change their ways

For the touch of mercy is sublime

Offers men a vision of the divine

Within the core of mercy is found

Goodness that covers most sins

It is the lifeblood of regeneration

That which brings renewal in life

Gift of Mercy (Cont'd)

To live humbly in faith thru mercy

Is to know that God is in control

It is to dwell close to love's heart

And to see in fullness of true light

End

Allotment of Mercy

Allotment of mercy is the best saved for last

Opens when the window of grace has closed

When all's exhausted with nothing to hang on

Save the unseen hand of divine Providence

It flows from the secret place of the father

To the faithful who have no other recourse

Demands that the believer show strong faith

To ask and to receive as his heart desires

Tis divine allotment for the matured in faith

As wine and pleasurable gift to lift the heart

For thru mercy comes the gift of the eternal

Such that do afford man goodness in life

❧✦❧

The pruned tree produces more thru mercy

As well the true shepherd worthy of the flock

Mercy is that which makes the way possible

For righteousness to bloom and branch forth

End

The Holy Ghost

Holy Ghost informs the chosen

From the place behind the veil

Into the heart of true believers

In all their walks and ventures

He does wake up the inner man

That dwells within each faithful

To prompt and encourage him

The power of anointing to use

So much stands in man's way

Battles to fight but not by flesh

Spirit within has been equipped

To handle all that bedevils life

The Holy Ghost (Cont'd)

Spirit within wields the sword

Calls forces of goodness together

To bring the wherewithal to fight

The evil that comes against man

All who rally to the good cause

Will be blessed in countless ways

Life's problems though they come

For such Providence makes a way

The flesh must be put on a leash

So the spirit can have full rein

To be charged up and ready to go

When the Holy Ghost makes a call

End

Garden of the Resurrected

Tis good and desirable indeed

To be counted with the certain

That God uses on certain days

To do wondrously among men

Certainty does   become   him

As man matures through faith

Growth from grace unto mercy

Fills him with divine anointing

Faithful who seeks after truth

In sincere love and not for gain

Is soon absorbed into true light

To wear life's crown of glory

He'll be entrusted with much

Of the treasured and hidden

For warm welcome awaits him

In garden of the resurrected

There he will find the priceless

With astonished joy and glee

The golden eggs thereabouts

Amid precious things of heaven

Wisdom and all the enduring

Eternal truths and knowledge

Things lost in the mist of time

All soon become his to possess

The veiled truth and mysteries

The seeds of creative impulse

Tis divine glory duly imparted

To the certain faithful in the way

From glory on to greater glory

As the divine urges man in love

To use the gifts entrusted to him

In aid of humanity's resurrection

End

By the Divine Dove

Death and gravity claim no hold

In the heavenly and starry places

For perfection is at work up there

In, around and through all things

Perfection sought appears close

But remains far and out of reach

Yet it beckons the seeker ahead

Becomes urge for progress of light

No man is perfect but only God

The faithful do come close enough

Thru the divine perfecting process

Availed man thru the Holy Ghost

He speaks little but says so much

To inform the attentive listener

So that he can be duly informed

And have all that he should have

The sons do have due knowledge

The manna needed for daily living

In tweets and updates received

From the dove of the Holy Ghost

Sent from wisdom's source above

To avail the faithful peace within

Shows him the issues to attend to

And traps of the enemy to avoid

Cannot be beguiled and misled

By contriving and conniving men

Not possible to deceive the son

Well informed by the Holy Ghost

End

Exalted Place of Wisdom

The heavenly father is ever faithful

In fulfilling all that he promises man

But the path that leads to his heart

Runs contrary to that of the world

To look for fulfillment in the world

Is to seek for life where there is none

Tis to run with the Gedarene herd

And sleep in the tomb with the dead

To take the winding trail less travelled

Is to walk with the divine in true love

Tis to walk by oneself but not be alone

And slip into new life via light's womb

Lonely path leads to the mountain top

Where the hidden and lost are found

And mysteries crystallize to be known

As dark night births the glorious dawn

Tis a nursery of the perfect and fulfilling

Where simplicity and orderliness attend

In a timeless vortex of creative impulse

Which wants not, hurries not or wastes

Quite an exalted place of living wisdom

And the nesting place of purified souls

Where all sing in love and dance in light

As events march to time's endless beat

End

Saga of Eternity

To do the impossible and overcome the world

Into place of increasing dawn and the limitless

Is to receive the desired passport of eternal life

Into realm of boundless and infinite possibilities

Master is in the disciple as father is in the son

Disciple is in the master as the son in the father

Worthy disciple can do more than the master

Yet the son can never be above the father

The master takes the disciple into truth and light

The disciple takes the old master into the new

Tis true and undying love realized thru eternity

In the saga of lives awake in resurrection's dawn

Saga of Eternity (Cont'd)

Master dies but lives on in the worthy disciple

As sons and fathers who take endless walks

In communal spirit within the halls of wisdom

As curators of humanity's collective goodness

The hushed voices of wisdom all blend together

Sages of the present and of ages gone before

Whispered truths that resound in noble hearts

In fleeting moments that dazzle as sunlight

The things that are pure do glow from within

To enlighten the way for all who seek after light

On eternity's trail paved with enduring truths

For hearts and minds filled with wisdom's love

End

Relays for Truth

Wisdom always justifies her offspring

And defines them as men for all ages

To them are the enduring gifts given

The fulfilling and everlasting that endure

Faithful custodians 'trusted with much

Are the seedlings for the regeneration

Stars of hope to be used as foundation

For the regime of new heaven on earth

The faithful ones do not speak for selves

As they point out the way to mankind

Just earthly voices who relay the truth

Whispered into their listening hearts

There are hidden obstacles in the way

Pits and traps that ensnare the unwary

As hope beckons to guide men into Life

On to the golden shores of the eternal

Destiny leads all the earmarked into Hope

Always a way for him who seeks in truth

Tis the marvelous beheld in time by men

When earthly voices tell heavenly truths

End

To be Worthy

Trapped in hopelessness

Blind and lost in the way

The battle for redemption

Is fought and won in spirit

In dimness or in the light

Spirit that dwells within

Can be truly ascertained

By state of man's affairs

The man that is faithless

Relies on his own might

State of home and estate

Speak to many battles lost

Faith tuned to the divine

Is the key to victory in life

Aids man do the marvelous

Change his earthly estate

The father is the arbiter

But truth is the proofing

Takes the furnace of trial

To forge the worthy man

End

Curators of the Unchanging

Sons of heaven do walk humbly on earth
In charitable living and in selfless sacrifices
As curators of the unchanging and enduring
Who share truth tried and proven in fire

Men who pollinate humanity with goodness
As givers and receivers from the spirit of Life
Who feed on and share the bread of truth
And drink from the spring of living water

Anonymous travelers on the earthly route
With life springing up in and around them
Obscured to the faithless yet much ablaze
In starry brilliance to all the faithful seekers

⟨❋⟩

Lust of the flesh and earthly possessions

Tis the cause for the blindness of mankind

Beclouds and debases the spirit of man

To blind and preclude from knowing truth

End

The Good Thing

Narrow and winding is the trail

Path on which goodness dwells

Broad enticing way of the world

Thereon evil masquerades as good

A caution to all that flock to buy

Beware of the world's promises

Her way is to sugarcoat things

To beguile and delude the mind

Good is not the easy and sweet

But that which endures to fulfill

Good thing in life may be bitter

But the offspring is ever sweet

The Good Thing (Cont'd)

The good thing demands sacrifice

To initiate and then to maintain

Goodness is built on a foundation

Of truth, good care and purpose

Good thing that taxes man so much

Is not of vanity but of humble stock

Pays back profitably in its due time

Always fulfilling and ever enduring

End

Crown of Thorns

Tis good indication of his love for God

When the world turns against a man

The one that was once loved by many

Becomes despised in the eyes of most

Closer to the heart of God a man gets

Stranger he becomes to most everyone

But his love and compassion for others

Become stronger despite the reproach

Loving sacrifices that truth demands

The life laid down for one's friends

In an effaceable and selfless manner

Tis the way of love and the call of faith

In labors without any acknowledgement

Amid good seeds planted in obscurity

Love's handiwork does blossom in full

And is known only in harvest season

The sacrifices that only a few can make

Is part of the cross that the faithful carry

And the test that faith demands of man

So he can climb up the heavenly steps

The man of sorrows and silent tears

First is the crown of the clown for him

Taunts and mockery do attend him early

Ere he can wear God's crown of glory

End

Not the Old

⚜

Images and impressions of the old-man

Stuck in the mind prove hard to erase

Friends and family are the last to 'see'

That a new man has emerged to stay

The faithful soon comes to understand

Tis part of the divine plan and purpose

To teach him the patient ways of hope

And about love that never gives up

God loves the faithful for hurts suffered

All that he endures without complaints

Valuable lessons about hope and love

Essence of godliness imparted to man

Not the Old (Cont'd)

Tis par for course in spiritual ascension

For the world walks by sight not by faith

Light sent into that place of darkness

Is not easily comprehended thereabout

The sons of light are an inconvenience

Some nuisance tolerated by the world

Men gone peculiarly strange and odd

Before the disbelieving eyes of mankind

To lack the spy glass of faith is to view

The new through the prism of the old

Tis inability to savor the taste of the new

But be stuck in stale and sour of the past

Not the Old (Cont'd)

Many who are in the proximity of light

Dismiss same and take it for granted

Yet few who are far do catch the vision

And see the beacon of hope that it is

Unable to separate the new from the old

The blind mistake the reborn for dead

But the new nature differs from the old

Much like a butterfly does from a worm

End

Candle Lights of the Divine

The vaunted and revered scholarly systems

Gazes into shadows and reflections of light

But the sons of enlightenment are spawned

And woven together in living and loving light

Divine anointing is bestowed from above

Chosen not by intellect but by the heart

The sons have not gazed in its reflections

But have become immersed into pure light

Strong faith is found in truth, light and love

In the spiritual baptism of life's wilderness

Far from the presumptive and the limiting

Not through the conceited intellect of man

To walk in under-appreciated love by many

With no ill-will to bear towards any man

Tis because the faithful are fully reassured

With the exalted love of the divine father

Anointed to serve his divine purposes

They are ambassador spirits from above

Pollinating bees that help the promising

To become fruitful in the fullness of time

Men that lug the heavy cross in humility

As candle lights that withstand evil winds

Do bear good fruits ripe for divine harvest

For they draw others to the way of light

End

~ 41 ~

Mold of Mercy

All purified souls walk with same purpose

In full spiritual maturity as anointed ones

To bring true   light so the blind can see

And share the needful so others can have

Spiritual brotherhood of immortals souls

All bonded together in true commonwealth

As noble ones who live by the golden rule

And speak the language of truth in love

Same spirits yesterday, today and forever

Wrought from the mold of divine mercy

Men given as gifts by the heavenly Father

From the womb of Life to share the truth

End

~ 42 ~

Exalted in Love

To walk in ancient trails of custodial spirits

Tempered with the blood of sacrificial love

Is to be forged in light's crucible of truth

And be purified in spirit from base to pure

The purified in spirit do keep in good care

Their vessels for honorable use by God

Truths that other men are precluded from

Are theirs to know and in fullness to have

They're primordial seeds of every new age

Sanctified to serve the cause of the divine

Good souls kept by the heavenly father

Used to initiate the cause of regeneration

Exalted in Love (Cont'd)

Strangers in the world who are not of it

Woven from golden strands of the eternal

These rejected sojourners when embraced

Help many souls to find good purpose in life

These are men fit for the living congregation

Who are the vessels kept for greater honor

And held to a higher standard of judgment

Not as mere mortals but gods among men

He that is given the tools to do the amazing

Must honor the father's call and bring forth

For him will be works that shine before men

To the father's glory and heaven's acclaim

⁘

Tis a long great journey into regeneration

As the father sheds his glory on the sons

In endearing rewards and enduring blessing

For the pleasure of both heaven and earth

Works commissioned for God last for life

Those for the praise of men only for awhile

To walk in company of the exalted in love

Affords man wherewithal for eternal glory

End

There's a Mystic

Life and death issues

Do dwell in the spirit

Spirit arrives with life

Departs man to leave

The emptiness of death

There's a divine mystic

Found in the pairing of

The son and the spirit

That flows out of love

And sustains the living

There's a Mystic (Cont'd)

Then is a glorious mystic

That flows to create Life

By blessed communion

Of the heavenly Father,

The Son and the Spirit

Man has many maladies

Due to impure thoughts

That poisons well within

Divine makes for healing

But Glory makes for new

The impure does choke all

Both Divine and Glorious

It robs the essence of Life

Causes many to be infirm

Takes wholeness from man

Worship with a pure heart

With thanks to the Father

Opens Love's heart fully

For healing to be availed

So wholeness can attend

End

Free and Fulfilled

⁓⁕⁓

The sons of heaven all walk in light

Laborers in spirit and hopeful prayer

Warriors prepared and ready for duty

As called upon by the Spirit of Life

Men given to renew and to restore

The things that are depleted and dying

They refill the empty shelves of lives

And maintain the vessels of goodness

Such bring the enduring to replace

That which breaks down in the way

And quits when the job is not done

So well-doing and love weary no more

Free and Fulfilled (Cont'd)

From dregs of despair to ray of hope

An ever-ready spirit there to replace

That which will not last till fight's end

And gives up easily in life's battles

The uplifting divine wind from heaven

Comes in the season of regeneration

To revitalize the broken down things

With a glory greater than the former

Tis the spirit of the free and fulfilled

That brings the latter rain in its wake

When the land is starved and barren

To sow the seeds of the ever-lasting

End

Band of Brothers

Band of brothers in spiritual agreement

Led and shielded by the divine essence

Established through grace onto maturity

And now covered in goodness and mercy

Maybe of little consequence in the world

Saintly spirits who do not look the part

Are favorites on whom the father dotes

With tender mercies in loving affection

Souls that are co-joined with the divine

Do define the order of the new regime

As umpires given to make destiny's call

And judges to determine humanity's fate

Trees worthy of producing good fruits

In noble endeavors guided by divine will

Who take the high road in all matters

To establish the heavenly ways on earth

They walk in divine wisdom on the right

In narrow path of righteousness in light

As travelers and riders on wings of faith

To places where heaven and earth meet

Well informed when and where it counts

With insight into what needs to be done

Thru petitions and requests duly answered

Ordained to help men glimpse the divine

End

Better for the Vessel

The fullness of the riches of God

Are for saintly spirits and noble souls

To receive in good care and custody

For the benefit and enrichment of all

No one can choose the saintly life

Tis bestowed on man by the father

A divine calling for only the chosen

Noble vessels that yield to the Potter

World's way is a pot-shot of mishaps

Certainly not of truth, love and life

But from that tree of good and evil

That has bedeviled man from Eden

Better for the Vessel (Cont'd)

❦

Things heralded with much acclaim

Cheers, ovation and applause galore

In salute to progress and civilization

All end with regrets and recrimination

Disappointments mar his undertakings

As decadence and frustrations build up

Time and effort wasted for lack of faith

As man fights against the divine will

Tis better for that vessel which yields

To the wise potter that fashioned him

The father knows what's best for man

His place on earth and best role to play

End

~ 54 ~

The Good and Evil

⁓⁂⁓

The intoxicating beat of the world

Is a syncopation of good and evil

Tis the fruit of the forbidden tree

A little bite and be hooked for life

Good and evil intrinsically mixed

No separation of one from other

Hard for man to tell them apart

Blind as a bat as he has become

The masters of this world   know

How to mask evil to look like good

They know that men go for looks

And charm them through the eyes

The Good and Evil (Cont'd)

The evil shepherds do lack in love

And make slaughter of the sheep

They beguile and mislead the flock

With false promises hard to deliver

Motive and intention of the heart

Determines what is good and evil

Good deeds must always be done

For the welfare and benefit of all

Unbridled lust for fame and fortune

Amid clamors for name recognition

Should never be motivation to act

For such corrupt all man's endeavors

The Good and the Evil (Cont'd)

❦

Man's ravings and supersized ego

With its constant craving to be fed

His voracious desire to be praised

Has made the good rare among men

End

The Righteous Trees

Midwives do attend the birthing

Of men into the divine household

They help weary travelers to reach

The beckoning doorsteps of mercy

In the last leg of the grand trek

As weariness and doubt encroach

The sons of heaven stand guard

With encouraging voices to reassure

The uplifting company of the sons

As spiritual messengers of the divine

Aid the straggling and the struggling

The exhausted and empty on the way

They're brothers who reach out to kin

As buffers to shield from evil winds

In labors of love that help to bring in

The travelers into Providence' arms

It is surely and sorely needed help

As the sons of heaven lend support

In response to heaven's summons

With words that soothe and comfort

As welcoming arms of the upright

They make room for one more tree

That has come to join kindred spirits

In the abode of the righteous trees

End

Cloak of Wisdom

⸻❦⸻

Wisdom found in   age and experience

Can be entrusted to the worthy in spirit

Who has come into the realm of mercy

Even if he is young as men count age

The wise in spirit defies the limits of time

For he will be in covenant with the divine

The young in age who is faithful and true

Will be worthy to wear wisdom's cloak

He'll live in a place beyond man's flesh

And walk in the greater light of God

Where man's feet can never stumble

For space and time matter little there

Cloak of Wisdom (Cont'd)

❦

Wisdom that wears the cloak of youth

Has untied the leash that constrains man

Where the truth has made the spirit free

There is a living billboard for divine glory

End

Choice that Wisdom Offers

Man cloaked in wisdom must convey

True light that shows men the way

The enduring and fulfilling to choose

But the vaunting and wasteful to hate

Wisdom affords man life over death

Not the preserve of age or experience

It exists everywhere to serve humanity

In enlightenment and good conscience

Attends the young not saddled with age

Who's noble in spirit and worthy of trust

The sons of light matured in their youth

And daughters well-polished as pillars

Wisdom has chosen not to discriminate

Seeks that suitable and welcoming home

To cover with eternity's cloak emblazoned

With the crest of the lamb of sacrifice

Heart that receives divine wisdom well

And follows up with diligent obedience

Therein is where the showers of blessing

And tender mercies alight from above

End

Ascendant Spirit

The ascendant spirit has set the flesh at naught

To be welcomed into the divine fold as a son

Belongs nowhere but yet belongs everywhere

Belongs with no one but belongs with all men

Lives for all yet makes no demand on anyone

He loves all men but he loves God above else

His footsteps of love are the seed pods of life

This child of love walks on earth without fear

For he thinks, speaks, acts and serves all in love

To make the dying things find new life again

❧

Ascendant spirit that has overcome the world

Man that soars on the glorious wings of faith

Through the uplifting stream of the divine wind

Will not bed down in the heart of the earth

For his heart has found the heavenly home

End

Wisdom of Love

Life triumphant that snatches victory from death

Spawns countless offspring from the womb of life

Wherever the divine impulse governs man's will

In wisdom of love blended and distilled in time

Tis due wisdom that sets the imposing at naught

Insightful knowledge that speaks to the mountain

To move it out of the path of truth and light

So men can see and declare the goodness of God

It only asks the mind to be set on the things above

That men love each other as they love themselves

To uphold and live in the spirit of justice for all

So benevolence and kindness be not cast aside

End

The Standard of Reference

The man by whom God measures his fellows

Is called to be forgiving and merciful in life

Has more important things to do with time

Than let the blind throw him off his strides

The man by whom God measures his fellows

Thinks kingly thoughts and takes princely steps

Faithful guided to the heart of every matter

No longer gropes about blindly in the world

Truth, purity, simplicity, orderliness and peace

Bear joyful testimony that the faithful serves

In the course and cause of goodness in light

So the curse of darkness can amount to naught

End

From Man to Worm

Crowd pleaser's his name

Can be anything to anyone

No matter time or place

For he craves men's praise

He's bound to lose himself

And become the worm

That beds down in dust

For he has lost his spine

He parted ways with truth

No longer able to stand

For he has turned infirm

In trying to be liked by all

In the tangled web of life

The enemy poses as friend

Does beguile and mislead

Into traps to man's regret

Man that rejects the true

Invites darkness to come

A veil to obscure the light

Make night order of his day

End

Shadow over Life

The enemy of light is always at work

To becloud the minds of unwary men

Uses earthly cares and worries to dog

To cast shadows over the spirit of Life

Fear and doubt hinder the walk of faith

Takes the lens of the mind out of focus

So the faithful amidst the throes of life

Is no longer able to keep hope's trust

With each twist of fate and fiery trial

The believer that won't let go of hope

Does end up with the new and better

For good fortune greets him in the end

End

~ 70 ~

Light against Darkness

To be safe from damages and ravages

Things that destroy most men in life

To be at ease with peace in the heart

Is man's lot when he's reborn in Light

Locked in bitter and life long battle

Ordained from the foundation of time

Light and darkness can find no accord

Always has been and will ever continue

Light brings on life and dons a smile

Nature cannot wait to embrace its rays

Light calls all in nature to sing along

An ode to creation and all that's good

Light against Darkness (Cont'd)

❧

Darkness loves death and wears a frown

Holds nature in an apprehensive grip

Dons the mask of fear that douses hope

Aims to kill dreams of Creation's spawn

There's a wall in place to sort things out

Firmament of hope to save from death

Shield that separates light and darkness

With passage only by divine anointing

Quite a firm membrane of separation

That keeps life from the touch of death

Tis smaller than the eye of the needle

Yet quite easy for a camel to pass thru

Light against Darkness (Cont'd)

A sacrifice to make and a price to pay

For passage from darkness into the light

The wise man does sell all that he has

So he can pass from death on to life

End

The Eternal Heart

Realm of the eternal

Is the fullness of light

By faithfulness in way

Of truth, love and life

The faithful in the way

Do twinkle from within

An illumination is in him

In the man pure of heart

A star of hope is born

Beacon of light to others

Fed from wisdom's well

With life's eternal truths

Providence's always near

Never far from the pure

For goodness and mercy

Attend all twinkling hearts

End

Under Divine Illumination

Momentary prompts of divine inspiration

Spontaneous as lightning's fleeting moments

Tis sublime gift borne of the divine wind

For the faithful who is ready and waiting

Flashes of lightning appear ever so briefly

Enough to expose that cloaked in darkness

A brief revelation that's full of illumination

To help the traveler maintain true course

The guilty is gripped in the throes of darkness

In fear of the thunderous clap after lightning

For he is bound in spirit and cannot harness

Divine power to shred the veil of ignorance

⚜

But the free in spirit do get from now to then

Travel in thought by light from here to there

To effect the work of goodness in night or day

Conquer space and time in twinkling of an eye

The wisdom obtained from divine illumination

Comes in glimpses of hope in moments of time

From ghosts of the past and the already known

To reach and grasp tomorrow's reality today

From beyond the wall encircling man's mind

The divine essence comes into the moribund

In the kiss of love to bring back life and hope

To awaken from sleep into a glorious morning

End

~ 77 ~

Sower of Life

The breath of life that awakens the dead in Spirit

In anointed words that cause life to spring forth

Comes from him who has died and risen in spirit

That loves goodness and truth with all his heart

He reaps life anywhere to sow in kind everywhere

For life returns to him that passes same to others

The universe loves and makes room for all such

For the man that seeks and hopes for good in all

He's the noble in spirit but does not look the part

Who calls all the willing to like faith and fortune

For nothing is more important in life than Love

Not like the saintly without but hypocrite within

❦

Sower that plants the seeds of goodness in love

Has brought the light that keeps darkness at bay

To help the blind to see and the lame to walk

Lead the captive spirit to join in freedom's song

Man has to see before he can have a purpose

He has to walk before he can fulfill his dreams

Has to be awake in spirit to have true fulfillment

He that can do all that has indeed reaped true Life

End

Fruit of the Fig

The eater from the fig tree

Becomes the fruit of the fig

He has joined the grand feast

In true love and not for gain

Grasps the symbolic language

That veils the sacred truths

The key to understanding all

In life and divine mysteries

Such is life in God's kingdom

Few words that say very much

In truth that governs all things

And measures the faith of man

Fruit of the Fig (Cont'd)

To speak little but yet say much

Little tweets with much to tell

Hiding in the plain sight of all

For all teeth of wisdom to chew

Tis traceable to heaven above

But of much use on earth below

Tis language used by the Father

To communicate truth in light

With same the father speaks

To the sons that he will adopt

The language of light and love

That frames truth into pictures

Fruit of the Fig (Cont'd)

The pictures in the scriptures

Are for the eaters of the fig

Men remade like the father

And mete for the divine feast

End

Nectar of New Wine

❦

Essence of the fruit of the fig

Is the nectar of the new wine

Contained by the new bottles

Who delight in love and mercy

The new are molded in mercy

By hands of the divine potter

Who searches hearts of men

To choose who is fit and able

Tis fulfillment of his promise

And justification for wisdom

When mere mortals can hold

The nectar of divine wisdom

Nectar of New Wine (Cont'd)

⚜

From father to sons in mercy

As the passing of the former

And the beginning of the new

In eternity's firm handshake

End

Web of Father and Sons

❦

All who are awake in spirit

Are connected to the eternal

The father, the sons and all

Immersed in truth and light

Father's throne at the hub

Giving in mercy to the sons

Who receive with due thanks

To share with love and joy

The Father has it all to give

But only to the faithful will he

All who hope to have a share

Have wisdom's plea to heed

⁓❊⁓

Loiter not in life's dark alleys

Places where angels tread not

Cookies there do poison minds

To bewitch and corrupt souls

Much in the world works against

Man who lives by God's truth

'Strait' and confining is the path

That leads from coffin on to Life

End

Language of Truth

Universal language of truth
Simple as there ever was one
The language of this or that
Yes or no and dos or don'ts

Tis the language of the heart
Heard by the purified in truth
The upright and firm in spirit
Marked to hear the inaudible

Tis borne of the Holy Ghost
Tweets received in real time
To assure the sons of Heaven
The Holy Spirit is near to help

End

River of Life

River of life that's pure as crystal

Wisdom and prescient knowledge

That flows from heaven's throne

As stream to sustain the tree of life

The tree of life is the family of God

Sons of mercy all numbered there

Ever ready to serve the father's will

In good deeds from directed steps

Hooked up as nodes of creation

In the light that only truth sustains

To bring out things new but old

As informed in real and due time

⚜

But the faithless are overwhelmed

By knowledge of the good and evil

Such hearts have become junkyards

For expendable dross of the world

End

Of God and Heaven

The dynamo of the kingdom of heaven

Is father, the son and the Holy Ghost

The sons are   the Lamb of sacrifice

Acceptable and well received above

Holy Ghost is means to communicate

Between the Father and all the sons

Tis the medium of Light and Love

Audible to hearts tuned to the divine

The father's pride and touch of love

Imparts the sweet smelling fragrance

Tis the potion of divine healing power

Apportioned to the sons by divine will

The dynamo of the kingdom of God

Is the water, the blood and spirit

The living water of life from above

To the truly faithful through the sons

The heavenly truths in Light and Love

In faithful obedience is the blood shed

To him that truly lives by God's word

Will the spirit avail all that he desires

End

Destined for Honor

God's chosen are kept for his use

As custodians of precious seeds

Been destined for works of honor

And charged with due prudence

They're bestowed with the wings

That lift to the exalted heights

To place of the dew of latter rain

Where the best is saved for last

Seal of faith is a badge of honor

Tis to bring the living water of life

And induce many to see the light

In accordance with the divine will

Destined for Honor (Cont'd)

Always with due honor and thanks

To the faithfulness of divine love

That opens the spiritual eye of man

To begin to see in the true light

End

Realm of Fulfillment

The realm of eternal life can be known

With eye of the spirit that sees in Light

Tis a garden of trees laden with fruits

Where the father communes with sons

Garden where immortals take a walk

Amid knowledge and tools of creation

Where true fulfillment can be found

For joy and peace is there to be had

Tis fulfillment found at meeting point

Where heaven and earth kiss in love

For thereabouts in sweetest concord

Wisdom whispers man's purpose to him

Takes wisdom to endure in the way

On the long and winding walk of faith

Same calls the faithful into communion

So the creature can know his Creator

End

Together From Time

❦

The heart of the faithful in love
Is washed in pure light of truth
To come into that understanding
Which hungers after the divine

The impurities of an evil world
Keep many separated from God
Only when the soul is cleansed
Can man know the greatest love

Love is the force which wakes up
The dormant spirit asleep in man
To seek return to creation's womb
Source from where all came to be

࿇

Those who come home in love

Were once known by the Father

Kindred folk knit together afore

As one from foundation of time

End

Speaker in Truth

Speaks not for himself but in truth for all

Nothing but to bring men into God's light

Into the fold of mercy thru faith and love

Where life's troubles become mere trifles

The blood of sacrifice works much wonder

Where truth is spoken and taken to heart

Same power that sets the prisoner free

Gives him the strength to face the world

Tis painful and costly to reject world's way

Much price to be paid in scorn and hatred

But the spite and defamation of the blind

Do turn to admiration in course of time

The faithful in light that suffers for truth

Stands to gain much in the fullness of time

As the curses of men soon turn to blessings

In a life of goodness quite out of this world

End

The Crossroads

Mankind is in self-check

As harvest season looms

Tis the pivotal crossroads

Season for man to choose

To be certain in his faith

Mankind is on the edge

At very end of the ledge

As rug of grace is pulled

For its season to separate

The 'child' from the man

The Crossroads (Cont'd)

❧

Child that becomes a man

Learns to stand by grace

From baby held up in past

He'll come walking by self

As man upright in mercy

End

The Awakening

Lame that could not afore

The same can now walk

Blind that saw only trees

Judged men by their means

Now see men as they are

Confusion and dissolution

About ending of the world

Faithless are left to wonder

The redeemed already know

A separation will sort all out

The Awakening (Cont'd)

꧁꧂

Wheat to be parted from chaff

The saved from the unworthy

Tis evening in humanity's day

As destiny's bell begins to toll

And the clock chimes its last

Choice between life and death

In sad endings or tears of joy

Only the worthy before God

Who heeded the call to life

Can make it into new dawn

End

The Little One

Man much beloved by God

Is exalted in righteous ways

The blind may not yet know

But he is one for the ages

The   little   is   great   indeed

When fortune's kind to man

The heart that belongs above

Is attended   well by mercy

The anointing of the divine

By unseen hands thru faith

Is glory which was promised

And now delivered on time

The Little One (Cont'd)

What shall this man be called?

He's name is the manna of God

The little that keeps on giving

Is embodied in God's beloved

End

Learn to listen

In weakest moments

So clear and so certain

A voice of hope comes

To calm troubled waters

In the hopeless times

And the darkest hours

Then in boundless love

Tender mercies alight

The dark seasons repeat

As night follows the day

Only to let man know

He is little before God

In down moments of life

Is when hope is reborn

As man learns to trust

Life and   love reappear

Tis help in nick of time

Voice that tutors in hope

Still, calm and reassuring

That says ask to receive

Takes truth in the heart

To keep dimness away

For with light in the soul

All thoughts come to life

End

~ 107 ~

Love's Command

To be so loved by the Father

With pride and delightful joy

Is faithful love that commands

That man's wishes be fulfilled

From the deep and exhaustless

That's the treasure trove of love

Tender mercies of the divine

Attend the sons through life

The promised is well received

With thankful joy by the sons

As bitterness vacates the heart

Then sweeter comes to abound

Love's Command (Cont'd)

If forgiveness is from the heart

And all the wrongs are let go

Mercy will indeed rule the day

So wholeness can abound in life

End

Melody of Life

Sun always shines for all

With glee upon its face

Ever in joyful exuberance

With no sad tales to tell

The sweet melody of life

Plays the enchanting tunes

In dawn of each morning

As birds awake to tweet

Do not forget the flower

That cannot wait to unfold

In colors and sweet nectar

To say life is good indeed

Melody of Life (Cont'd)

꧁꧂

Sun's always eager to hear

A refrain of life's melodies

With flame of love in heart

Nothing can douse the 'sol'

End

The Simple Life

Needless things clutter man's life

With no room for good to abound

A deadly grip that chokes the spirit

So sickness and death can parade

The simple life in orderly living

Puts focus on the things above

With little of it on things below

So fulfillment can have the day

The true self that is at his core

Man can find by pruning his life

The part that responds to truth

Knows there's no shame in light

With clarity afforded by true light

Not in conformity with the world

From the edge of life's wilderness

The man reborn can do all things

End

In True Confession

Words become few and measured

When life is lived in true confession

For man that bears witness to truth

Speaks only the few words needed

Man called by certainty of truth

Is a spout of the wellspring of life

For living waters pour from hearts

That yield to the divine will in love

No longer by sight but only by faith

With room for goodness and mercy

At all times and all places in life

In obedience to divine commands

In True Confession (Cont'd)

❦

From the shadows into the full light

Confusion abates and fades away

As serenity reigns over man's soul

When true confession is life's credo

End

Lot for Each Son

❧

The potential to do great things

And model the right way of life

Is the lot of every faithful heart

With a plot appointed in kind

Life is the grand drama stage

An orchard to be cultivated

Where all should know and trust

That the truth sets the spirit free

The divine calls and mandates

Each son to be a director fit

To guide the believer on how

To play laudable parts in life

Lot for Each Son (Cont'd)

The sons know how to share

And the faithful hearts to guide

The father makes it all happen

As he's executive producer of all

The right script must be had

Light in triumph over darkness

And good to prevail over evil

Winning production in all times

The long running drama of life

Motion picture for those above

Tis apple of gold that's turned

'to silver pictures for all to see

Lot for Each Son (Cont'd)

The earing of divine wisdom

Decorates the attentive ear well

In words that are fitly spoken

To serve well all those who heed

In the urgent plea of the Father

And his anguished cries of love

He besieges all men to accept

Life's offer in reconciliatory love

End

The Silver Screen

The handiworks of the sons of Light

Are timeless works forever displayed

As golden directors come from above

To carry out the brilliant works below

The star lit night is the silver screen

In twinkling majesty for all to see

As mortals gaze in star struck awe

On the canvas for works well done

Tis glory of the father shed on sons

Who passed audition to star in roles

With different parts to play in life

But equal billing in true living color

The Silver Screen (Cont'd)

Part well played is much acclaimed

By the heavenly host as the audience

That watches, judges and records all

In truth, light and love for all eternity

Only those who gave all in love

Are deemed worthy to be exalted

To join the troupe of celestial stars

In the grand stage up in the sky

Index of credits is the book of life

As record of those heavenly acclaimed

Luminaries all who showed the way

For the blind below to see and follow

⁓⁂⁓

The heavenly way is best for man

Avails the divine anointing for him

To untie the knot and lift the veil

Makes the dead in spirit to live again

It shines light into darkened hearts

To chase away fears and torments

With truth that resoundingly declares

Great power rests in sacrificial love

End

Commonwealth of Love

Where God connects with the sons

Is a web of life pulsing with knowledge

What one knows the others can know

What one has the others can also have

Tis a commonwealth of brethren spirits

That clamors not for the praise of men

For their bliss is found in laboring for all

In sacrificial love that flaunts not self

Hunger for the spotlight and attention

Is like an overwhelming flood over men

The faithful are shielded from its deluge

For it makes road-kill of unwary souls

A solid rock is the anchor for the soul

That knows the right and does the same

Always on right path and due knowledge

In worthy service always noticed above

End

Escape from the Past

Father watches from above

As the sons perform for him

With the eager eyes of love

His anointed ones to admire

They keep the unclean at bay

And put all the impure away

So to escape viral impulses

That pull back to the past

When light is not embraced

Then seduction will lead away

To slippery domain of shadows

Where darkness is not afar off

⁓❊⁓

Tis the subterranean pit below

The dark basement of life itself

Where the angels fear to tread

And the decrepit make a home

Each son must be on guard

Unequal yoking is the bane

That takes away from man

The life that he could've had

Man that lets the past alone

The dead to bury the dead

To live with the seeds of hope

Soon reaps the new and fresh

End

Confused and Faithless

The unclean feasts in the heart

Of unworthy not true to faith

That professes loudly before all

Just for show in false confession

He picks and chooses to suit

What to obey and when to do

Ruled by the spirit of caprice

With eyes for the praise of men

Good one day but not the next

With troubles that rift the soul

Deeply conflicted and torn apart

In the domain of the unstable

A bipolar existence is for him

The confused and faithless soul

He neglected the steady rock

And built on the shifting sand

End

The Divine Vehicle

He that has been entrusted

To drive the divine vehicle

Must carry along other men

To join him on the 'omnibus'

All are free to come aboard

If they abide by God's words

For faith in the power of truth

Is the token that all must pay

The driver anointed is like a sun

All who join him are the planets

Who obey willingly and lovingly

In a marriage of faithful souls

The Divine Vehicle (Cont'd)

The sun always gives to him

Who opens to warm embrace

Offers up the life giving rays

To anyone who fears not light

The bridegroom does attract

Maidens to bear his children

As planets that harbor 'lives'

Seeds 'trusted to their wombs

The maidens that bear children

Regeneration belongs to them

With essence of the everlasting

And the divine wrapped within

No longer will death be an end

Only new life out of the former

For better comes from the old

In the splendor of regeneration

Offspring of the father's love

Goodness shielded and saved

Tis water poured into maidens

That turns into cherished wine

End

Harmony through Peace

All things do talk to the other

When harmony is found in life

For there is a creative order

That underlies all thru universe

Tis the consciousness of life

That speaks in one voice to all

To tear down veil of darkness

So the dead can wake in light

There is an ear in the heart

That lives to please the father

Such is tune with the divine

And will not stumble in life

To live in certain peace within

Is to room above in the spirit

So storms of life can become

Mere ripples that pass away

Peace that dwells in the heart

Is platform on which to stand

And receive with thankful joy

The enduring gifts from above

Peace within anchors the soul

Holds the key to fortune's door

Man that has no peace within

Has his portion with confusion

End

The Plain and the Secret

Praise and thanksgiving to the Father
Yield much from store of Providence
In knowledge and wisdom that shines
From Illumination's womb way beyond

The divine storehouse is readily opened
To grant the desires of faithful hearts
The plain and the secret to behold
Things hidden from foundation of time

In special offerings from Benevolence
As he shows his magnanimous hands
To faith wrought thru willing obedience
By the love that never fails to bless

The Plain and the Secret (Cont'd)

❦

How wondrous his goodness can be

Wisdom's apple become silver pictures

Gifts of the father to his beloved sons

For whom   he reserves mercy's best

End

~ 134 ~

The Divine Bond

The offering of praise

Thanksgiving in grace

Leads to a quiet life

Into a place of peace

Tis blessings that lend

And holiness that begs

A soberness of mind

In moderation of flesh

Power laden within

Moves fortune's tide

To always propagate

With goodness in wake

The Divine Bond (Cont'd)

❧

The Arbiter of fate

Does entrust much

To the noble souls

With hearts of gold

In sweet doting love

And in abiding trust

Goodness for hearts

Set on things above

To never abandon or

Forsake the beloved

Is the good promise

Love makes in faith

End

The New Dawn

Regeneration begins at point of escape

From the misguided and misgiven past

Tis like the welcome face of dawn

A break that follows an unending night

The light of the pure and true is ideal

For the seeds loaded with goodness

As no other manner of seed will thrive

Under the judgment of dawn's new light

Its light is the indisputable evidence

That the grand awakening has begun

Faithful that waited in hopeful belief

Soon become witness to sweet relief

The New Dawn (Cont'd)

Such that kept good watch in true vigil

Have received the means for the rebirth

In divine power to be duly displayed

As the golden-hearted rule the day

End

Destiny's Sons

◈

Tis hope that affords the faithful

The means to effect much good

The power to switch on the light

So mankind can see in fullness

One son can chase a thousand

An adequate number of them

Is grand that changes the world

In power of a great divine wind

There is a star-search going on

The father always keeps watch

As he chooses and adopts sons

Into divine's ordained household

Chosen from all over the earth

Different manner of fruit is borne

By the tree of life each month

To add to the count of the sons

Different countries and skin colors

Differing tribes and babel tongues

But tis the same within each heart

For therein God makes his home

End

Dance of Time

❧

Together just like binary stars

The sons are paired in twos

To conjure a divine spearhead

That pierces through any wall

In the bond between the sons

Tween the elder and younger

Wisdom finds the ample room

For blissful harmony to attend

In the full measure of time

As the young becomes the old

The old is reborn as the young

So life can swallow up death

Dance of Time (Cont'd)

⚜

Spiritual bond between the two

Is youth replenished by wisdom

Behold eternity is in full display

In this perennial dance of time

End

Wonder of Rebirth

Hourglass and figure eight
Iconic emblems of rebirth
One half fills up the other
To begin the count anew

Matter soon changes face
And energy changes form
Hushed silence everywhere
At the wonder of rebirth

Alas the debased is purified
So the exalted can emerge
In bubbles of hopeful joy
A new is displayed in dawn

Wonder of Rebirth (Cont'd)

Under God's divine sunshine

Everything does get better

From the less to the greater

In the full passage of time

End

Urge to Perfection

Elder and young in faith

Form an irrepressible duo

That urges on the spread

Of truth and light in love

Each bears up the other

As all share in strength

One to his fellow in love

So no one is left without

Tis recipe for the perfect

When the imperfect things

Are well blended in love

With a pinch of divine salt

Search for the perfect

Always seems at hand

Yet remains out of reach

To urge on light's spread

Wisdom of the highest

Does make things better

To turn human weaklings

Into pillars of strength

Tis an eternal sunshine

When hearts join as one

As flames fused thru love

In a reach for perfection

End

The Self-Examined Life

Tis the season of pre-judgment

Time of self-examination for all

Window of grace is soon to close

So mercy's door can open fully

Indolence may come from grace

For it is often taken for granted

But vitality comes from mercy

For one has to ask to receive it

The unworthy gets stuck in grace

As apathy soon takes hold of him

All are not ordained for mercy

Yet none that pleads is denied life

The Self-Examined Life (Cont'd)

Many goats lurk in the sheepfold

Enthralled with feeding the flesh

There'll be no room left for such

When the rug of grace is pulled

All becomes known in true light

In the judgment of the noon day

For then there is no place to hide

From the shame and guilt of sin

The soul that has not known truth

That finds reason to hope again

Will strive to change his ways

And wake up while there is time

Many more are lost meanwhile

Hogs that suffocate in their stuff

As blind men not yet able to see

That things do possess the soul

End

For the Pure in Heart

Kingdom of light is the realm of truth

Where one can know as one is known

For the pure in heart who live by truth

The field of dreams does open in full

But for hearts wherein darkness lurks

The amazing remains forever closed

For experiences of the kingdom of light

Are not for the impure of heart to see

Clearly perceived by purified hearts

Pictures sent from the womb of light

Totally unknown to darkened hearts

As dimness of soul precludes receipt

❦

Kingdom of God is the place of refuge

Wherein enlightened spirits are uplifted

But the world's kingdom is a subterfuge

Where all the faithless lay down in dust

End

In Total Trust

The day unfolds and the Spirit leads

Begins at dusk and breaks in dawn

All thru the night until slumber ends

In grand smile to frame God's face

The long trek on the journey of faith

Has to be taken to the glorious end

Tis the better way above all else

For eternity's gift is at par with none

God never fails to deliver as due

Always does finish what he starts

Brings the well-tended to full harvest

For those who trust and obey his will

He leads In the path of patient hope

In unexpected ways not understood

Always the amazing and best result

When the venture comes to an end

It takes a maze to get the amazing

Faith calls all to trust and let God

To pray and sing along is best to do

For man in communion with Hope

End

The Cornerstone

Man is reborn to fit all seasons

As an all-cast received everywhere

But an outcast among his own

Who reject and revere not truth

The tragedy of willful blindness

Borne of living by sight not faith

Sad mistake the ignorant make

Who judge books by their cover

The truly wise judge the content

A man may look sublime without

But deep within will lack in virtue

Man of means yet empty inside

The Cornerstone (Cont'd)

The wise are blamed for the woes

Made scape goats for sins of many

The people's guilt on the innocent

Is proofing of the Lambs of sacrifice

The rejected is soon sought after

As the destined given to become

The cornerstone of every building

Without which nothing can stand

End

Buyer Beware

Wisdom that speaks to the heart

Does not change in tone or tune

But spirit that beguiles the flesh

Changes pitch to suit the sale

Offers man this but sells him that

Promises fulfillment to one and all

In deceitful ploys that delude many

And amount to weariness of flesh

In floods that deluge man's mind

With more than he can manage

Always besieging him with wants

In one flawed choice after another

Buyer Beware (Cont'd)

If this does not suit man's fancy

Then the other will be the candy

If the sour does not suit the palate

Then the sweeter will cut the cake

Counsel for vainglorious appetites

Let the unwary   buyer be aware

Promises to deliver much for little

Always end up as good for nothing

End

The Little Place

⁓⁂⁓

The place of the little things
Destined to produce the great
Tis seed of Ephraim set aside
For him beloved by the divine

Chosen in favor over the rest
By the hand of Love's blessing
To him the best is rendered
Tendered as delightful mercies

Ingredients for all his wishes
Always there at hand for him
He who seems to have little
Soon has all his garners full

Only for the humble in spirit

Who gives God the due glory

For wisdom borne of the divine

Leaves no room for vain glory

End

Little covered by Love

The place of the little lone tree

On the edge of life's wilderness

Increases in strength and beauty

As time takes unperturbed steps

Its height will kiss the heavens

Branches will touch the horizons

The lone tree is in Ephraim's lot

And covered by love thru time

Places abuzz with glitter and glitz

Festooned to please man's flesh

And dull the spirit within him

There the popular crowds flock

Such is not the lot of Ephraim

For therein the heart is the light

With God's right hand ever near

To bless the little covered by love

End

The Garden

The spirit of the divine dwells not

In noisome and disorderly places

It is in the quiet and peaceable

That the true and pure is found

A garden frames a good picture

Of that quiet and peaceful place

Therein is where divine's purpose

Proceeds in good orderly conduct

A garden is the ideal place where

Nature displays in lovely showcase

Place for man to watch and learn

The unhurried pace of the divine

The Garden (Cont'd)

﹏❀﹏

No stampedes to wreck life there

In hurried stumbles of uncertainty

Nothing is wasted for all is good

In favorite place of the divine Spirit

End

Matured in Faith

The milk is for the young

Just starting on the way

He has no teeth to grind

Digest the meat of truth

Season comes in the life

Of the young in the way

Maturity calls out to say

Time to become a man

The time will never come

Unless the young is suited

To tune out and turn off

Foolish impulses of youth

Matured in Faith (Cont'd)

⚜

Tis then the roots of faith

Find anchor on solid rock

So the child can step up

To be chiseled into a man

End

Eye on the Housetop

Man whose spirit dwells up on the housetop

Has a good vantage point from wisdom's perch

With eyes fixed above he can discern the future

And reach the horizon to bring near the new

Brings much into light from around the corner

Things hidden from view so the seeker can know

An exalted perch for man to learn from wisdom

How things should be when true love abounds

Eye on the housetop is awake in the true Light

Unlike those who dwell below and are still asleep

They're bottom dwellers who settle in the house

The earthbound who care not for room above

⁓⁓⁓

The perch on the housetop is man's only refuge

Spirit not focused above lacks in due knowledge

Lives in willful blindness and does not yet realize

That an overwhelming flood licks at the doorstep

End

The Bridge

No matter how sincere the milk is

It's just there to help babies grow

Only needed in the infant season

And the slumbering days of youth

Child that must become a man

Soon or later will have to know

Milk is there to serve as a bridge

To nourish him till youth be past

Takes meat to mature into a man

Teeth and grit for those who chew

Babies reproduce after themselves

But a man bears a son like himself

The Bridge (Cont'd)

Many desire the watered down

Much harder to tell such the truth

Frozen in fear and mired in doubt

The sweet and easy is all they love

Across the bridge man must go

May crawl on his hands and knees

From here to there to rid the fear

There to stand and claim the prize

Prize is knowledge in the true light

For lack of which many do perish

The man who has it rises in time

To find ample room in God's heart

End

No Use for Bitterness

The matured with teeth and grit

Who can digest the meat of truth

And give the gift of forgiveness

Turns the bitter into sweet victory

Gift of mercy from man's heart

Releases the spirit within to soar

With guilt from the past removed

Much more become possible in life

The spirit within that's been freed

Has been fitted with wings of glory

He'll ride the wind in divine mercy

To be lifted unto an exalted realm

⟨✦⟩

Eternal being with God's anointing

Immortal soul with a song in heart

Borne of light from the womb of life

In escape from the shadow of death

Mercy gives and yet receives back

It lends the updraft that lifts up high

Tis the essence of the divine wind

That never fails to rise when needed

Life under mercy's tender showers

Comes about when all's been forgiven

Then is no use for salt of bitterness

But healing balm to awaken new life

End

With Abiding Love

The great power of love

As witnessed through light

Does the amazing in life

In works that truly shine

Breakers of new grounds

In manners not done 'fore

By visions and strong faith

Enabled to do all thru love

Wisdom gives much in love

The faithful able to receive

Is called to share with all

And sow in labors of love

Like combs of the honey

In ever fulfilling sweetness

Tis a delicacy for the soul

When love gives her feast

Man grafted to the divine

Same is fixed and secure

Only takes what he needs

Always with abiding love

End

The Backpack

An oversized backpack in life

Will weigh heavily on man

Smaller one with the needed

Helps to ease life's burdens

Good choices along the way

Made to pare the worldly

Lightens man's load in life

To spare him troubles ahead

An easy yoke in life does well

Helps man be worthy of grace

So his spirit is always tuned

To hear the still voice of hope

The Backpack (Cont'd)

Hope makes worthy sacrifices

As seeds of goodness sown

Soon to be harvested in time

As blessings that abound in life

End

Shame of the Cross

The gift of immortality

Home among the stars

To walk with the 'gods'

An offer many decline

The broiling in the fire

The shame of the cross

Tis the needed token

That most refuse to pay

From darkness 'to light

Something has to burn

Takes the flesh and ego

To make perfect fodder

✦

The cross declares to all

Any who cares to know

In heaven or earth below

The father reigns supreme

He crowns all men in love

Who uphold light in truth

To keep darkness at bay

And help mankind to see

The faithful labors in love

Under the obscured self

Brings the infusion of life

To halt the curse of death

❧❀☙

The anointing in the Spirit

Only by shame of the cross

An irreversible gift to have

That only the Father gives

End

The Wine Bearer

⚜

Destiny calls for willing hearts and ready hands

For laborers worthy to change humanity's face

The vine that will produce sweet wine in time

Requires good and tender care until harvest

By his commitment to serve others in true love

Man's endeavors send out a heavenly invitation

For he has made his earthly lot to be pleasing

So God can stroll in the garden of his heart

A life and place resorted to please the Father

Evokes the serenity of the blissful and divine

Impulses of goodness dictate all actions there

And urges all willing believers to follow suit

The Wine Bearer (Cont'd)

✦

Man anointed with sweet smelling fragrance

Who models and translates heavenly virtues

Brings the new wine that requires time to savor

In offerings of love so men can taste the better

End

The Grand and Little

⚜

From a divine impulse all things came

Man must never be deluded otherwise

An all-knowing wisdom did create it all

The son that knows can create as well

As the father does good sons can too

Like cookies baked in the same mold

The colors vary but the process is same

Takes time, water, heat and pressure

The same yesterday, today and forever

Sons remade in the image of the father

To remake earth in the order of heaven

Same mind and motif diligently at work

The Grand and Little (Cont'd)

❧

'Little' heavens being created on earth

With divine aesthetics still in command

In the grand as well as in the little plot

Only difference being in scale and size

The divine motivation never changes

Transformation in soul, mind and body

To serve and give man foretaste of glory

And afford him very good days on earth

To him bestowed with the divine mind

Will be sublime and blissful moments

It's all there waiting for man to have

Thru the anointing of the Father on sons

End

The Sons save the Day

The works of the sons never stop

An endless cycle of commuting

To bring the heavenly to all men

From realm above to here below

God's chosen do rise in spirit

And venture to exalted heights

To soak up the dew of wisdom

Laden clouds that bear the rains

Man with the pitcher of water

Pours the precious from above

Refreshing gifts from the divine

So the starved can have new life

Patched souls that dwell below

Devoid of life sustaining waters

Only the sons can save the day

To the delight of those who wait

Prescient knowledge and wisdom

As living water from the divine

Issue forth from mercy's throne

For the sons to receive and share

End

In Destiny's Command

❦

The still small voice of the divine confides

In faithful promise never to disappoint man

Tells him not to weary or give up in the way

When there's much good work left to be done

The faithful under Destiny's will and command

Yields in spirit so his flesh can take the steps

There's progress on to victory for the obedient

That trust in divine will as life's guiding star

Divine's face is always framed with a smile

When man labors for goodness and not for gain

Such is shielded from misdeeds and stumbles

Kept immune from the bedeviling in the world

In Destiny's Command (Cont'd)

The long dark night does end in morning delight

For honey and glory come from challenges met

Victory comes in due season thru patient hope

As man learns to hear, speak and walk in wisdom

End

A Feast for Hogs

⁂

The mighty wind of the Spirit

Urges humankind to choose

To reject the way of the world

And take the righteous path

Churches of bricks and mortar

Are not arbiters of man's fate

A place to begin faith's walk

For those who seek after truth

Opportunism rules hearts there

As vultures devour the unwary

In ploys to feed on men's guilt

While caring little for their souls

Culprits in the abuse of grace

Who null the anointing of God

As the glitter of silver and gold

Dulls the light of Christ therein

Many do compromise the truth

And abuse God's grace for cash

Charity no longer rule the day

For it is become a feast for hogs

End

Sharing the True

⚜

Rendezvous with the divine

Is not in buildings or groups

Only on the long lonely walk

And that is the gospel truth

The bond with the divine

For those who seek to know

And are willing to be told

Takes place by one on one

To share the truth is hard

It falls mostly on deaf ears

Those with the will to share

Are certain and strong in love

For his works to be sublime

And shine before all eyes

The faithful must play a part

To help mankind see the Light

End

The Blessed Man

The misinformed man believes

But it is quite far from the truth

That material prosperity is proof

A man's way is pleasing to God

Tis welcome when goods abound

If not tainted by lust and greed

Rewards exist and also blessings

A big difference between the two

Reward is okay but much limited

A blessing is a far different matter

In multiple ways and many areas

A blessing is a gift that never ends

Only the blessed man is attended

By rare gifts of goodness and mercy

As window of heaven's never closed

For the faithful man truly blessed

A blessing is a binding covenant

True and faithful companion in life

Tis not bound by season or place

Ageless when hearts beat for God

End

An Intimate Means

There is an intimate means

By one loving heart to another

The father uses to commune

With the faithful in the way

Means for the father to fold

Loving arms around his own

He's the Holy Ghost from above

That only the father can send

Tis for those with ear to hear

In the gesture that speaks to say

I am now with you through life

Never to leave or abandon you

A sure affirmation for those

Exalted from grace unto mercy

Given to comfort and show man

A grand way to a higher plane

The higher is Heaven's tableland

A place to join the conversation

What more is there to seek for

Than to be privy to mind of God

End

A Higher Calling

There's a momentous season in life

In man's journey through the earth

Destiny calls him to make a choice

Tis a test of faith many see as fate

A divine affirmation comes to bear

Some are chosen but others are not

As higher purpose and greater calling

Comes to prevail in humanity's cause

The chosen found worthy before God

Are the heralds who begin the new

Vanguards of the eternal spring of life

Under the banner of peace and love

New visions in a greater illumination

Thru obscurity by voluntary humility

A higher way borne of the golden rule

For those guided by the Holy Ghost

The challenging moments define man

To add up to his finest hours on earth

So higher calling and greater purpose

Can become the calling card of his life

End

Goodness is not the easy and sweet

But that which endures to fulfill

It may be bitter in the beginning

But the offspring is ever cherished

OTHER BOOKS BY KALU ONWUKA INCLUDE-

(Poetry)

In Enchantment of Eternity

Capsules of Divine Splendor

Tones of the Stellar

(Books for Spirit, Mind and Body)

Nuggets of Resurrection

Pulses of the Divine Heart

Etching for the Faithful Heart

No Hurry to Horeb

(Quotations and Insights)

Inspiration Fountain

All titles are available as paperbacks or e-books and may be purchased at many retail outlets/distribution channels. The titles may also be purchased through Granada Publishers at **granadapublishing.com.** In addition, excerpts of the author's works can be read through his website at **kaluonwuka.com.**

Kalu Onwuka is a prolific author who writes about faith walk in this new age of man's spiritual awareness. His books offer tit-bits on how to find a balance between the earthly and heavenly. He is a man of many accomplishments and draws inspirational insights from experiences in many areas of life. He is a *Teacher, Poet, Lyricist, Electrical Engineer and Entrepreneur.* He is married, a father of five and lives in Southern California.

He is the author of the *On the Golden Strand* series which are encapsulations of both spiritual and earthly experiences on the walk of faith. These include *Nuggets of Resurrection, Pulses of the Divine Heart, Etching for the Faithful Heart and No Hurry to Horeb.* He is also the author of the *Poems in Faithfulness to the Divine* Series which are books of poetry and songs. These include *Anthems in the Glorious Dawn, In Enchantment of Eternity, Tones of the Stellar and Capsules of Divine Splendor.*